GO FACTS ENVIRONMENTAL ISSUES
Endangered Animals

A & C BLACK • LONDON

Endangered Animals

© 2006 Blake Publishing
Additional material © A & C Black Publishers Ltd 2007

First published in Australia by Blake Education Pty Ltd.

This edition published in the United Kingdom in 2007 by
A & C Black Publishers Ltd, 38 Soho Square, London, W1D 3HB.
www.acblack.com

Hardback edition
ISBN 978-0-7136-7960-1

Paperback edition
ISBN 978-0-7136-7968-7

A CIP record for this book is available from the British Library.

Publisher: Katy Pike
Editor: Mark Stafford
Design and layout by The Modern Art Production Group

Photo credits: p5 (tc), p7 (bl, br), p11 (b), p15 (t), p17 (all)–AAP;
p5 (b)–Image Quest Marine.

Printed in China by WKT Company Ltd.

This book is produced using paper that is made from wood grown in managed sustainable forests. It is natural, renewable and recyclable. The logging and manufacturing processes conform to the environmental regulations of the country of origin.

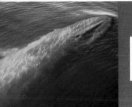

Endangered Animals

Wild animals that are close to **extinction** are known as **endangered**. Many animals are endangered because their habitats have been destroyed, or they are hunted in great numbers.

Loss of homes

The main reason for the decline in animal numbers is loss of natural **habitat**. The forests, grasslands, oceans and wetlands where animals live are damaged or destroyed by humans – the animals can no longer find enough food, water or shelter.

Tropical forests contain more than 50 per cent of the world's animal and plant species, but the rate of forest destruction is at its highest ever. Farms and livestock are replacing wild animals and forests; rivers and waterways are polluted by farming and industry.

Hunting

Some animal **species** become endangered by hunting and **poaching**. Rhinoceroses are hunted for their horns, and whales are hunted for their meat. Other animals, such as tigers and leopards, are hunted for their skins. Some animals are killed because they damage crops or harm **domestic** animals. Animals are also hunted for sport.

Some people are trying to protect endangered animals. Natural habitats can be preserved by including them in wildlife reserves. Endangered species such as giant pandas and tigers are bred in zoos, and some species can be returned to their natural habitats.

Gouldian finch

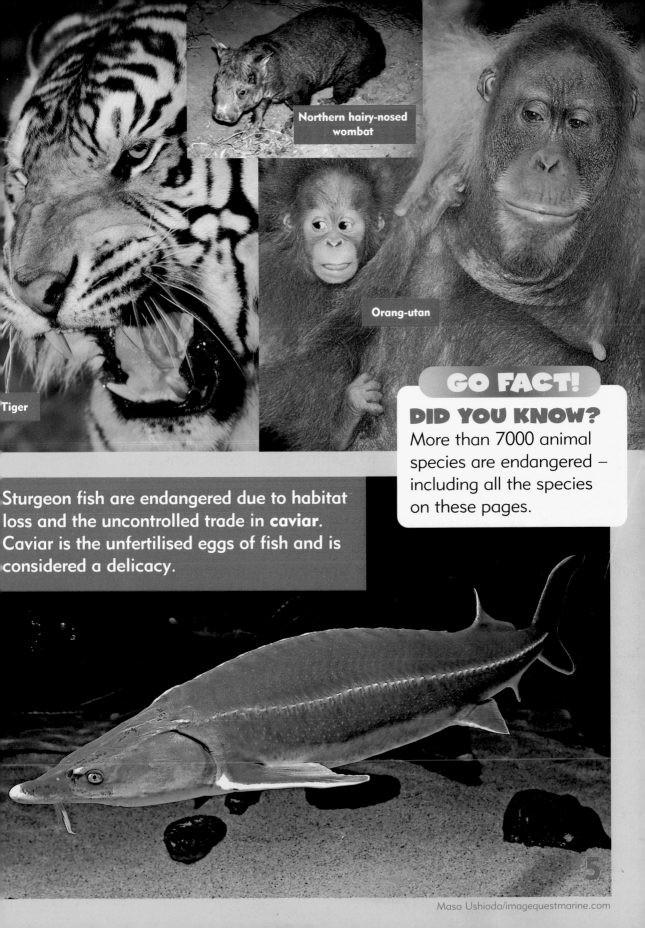

Northern hairy-nosed wombat

Orang-utan

Tiger

Sturgeon fish are endangered due to habitat loss and the uncontrolled trade in **caviar**. Caviar is the unfertilised eggs of fish and is considered a delicacy.

5

Masa Ushioda/imagequestmarine.com

Extinction

Extinction is not just something that happened the dinosaurs. Many animal species have become extinct in the past 50 years.

The last ibex

One of these is the Pyrenean ibex, a species of goat that lived in the rocky, mountainous regions of Spain and southern France. The number of animals fell below 100 due to hunting in the 1800s. Numbers continued to fall, probably due to competition for food with other species, poaching and diseases caught from domestic animals. In 1981, the population was down to only 30 animals.

The last known Pyrenean ibex was found dead on 6 January 2000, crushed by a fallen tree in a national park in Spain.

Disappearing frogs

The most serious wave of extinctions taking place is of frog species – up to 122 species have become extinct since 1980.

One entire family of frog specie the gastric-brooding frogs from Australia, has died out.

Scientists believe a fungal disease and **global warming** are the main causes of the frog extinctions.

Bilbies hanging on

Sometimes an introduced anima endangers other species by becoming a **predator** or competing for food. In the mid 1800s, Australia introduced foxes which became predators of the native bilbies, a species of bandicoot. Then rabbits were brought in a few years later and they competed with the bilbies for food. The lesser bilby is now extinct, and the greater bilby is endangered.

In the UK, the native red squirrel is endangered by competition with grey squirrels introduced from North America.

The Nubian ibex, related to the extinct Pyrenean ibex, is endangered by hunting, habitat damage and competition with livestock.

GO FACT!

DID YOU KNOW?

At Currawinya National Park in Queensland, an area of 25 square kilometres has been fenced off to protect bilbies from predators, and to allow the bilbies to breed and grow in number.

Tigers

Tigers are endangered because of poaching and habitat destruction.

Bengal tiger

Siberian tiger

Sumatran tiger

Loss of species

In the past there were eight species of tiger in Asia. Today there are only five species left, all of which are endangered. The decline in tiger numbers is due to the illegal trade in body parts, habitat destruction and because locals consider them pests.

Tigers live in thick forests, grasslands and swamps, and mostly eat deer and wild pigs.

They also eat fish and birds. Humans clear and settle the land where tigers hunt. As a result, tigers find it more difficult to find food and move closer to farms and villages in search of prey. If a tiger kills a domestic animal for food, farmers hunt the tiger and kill it.

Poachers

Tigers are also hunted by poachers who want their skins and body parts. Poachers kill tigers in traps or with poison, to avoid damaging the skin with a bullet hole. Tiger skins sell for large amounts. The body parts, including bones, claws and eyes, are used in Chinese and Korean **traditional medicines**. Some people believe that tiger body parts will cure sickness and bring them good luck.

Tiger species	Estimated number in the wild
Bengal	3000–4000
Indochinese	1000–1700
Sumatran	400–500
Siberian	200
South China	30
Caspian	EXTINCT
Java	EXTINCT
Bali	EXTINCT

Tigers are successful in only one or two attacks out of every 20.

The tiger's 10 centimetre-long claws stay sharp because they remain retracted inside its paws when not hunting.

DID YOU KNOW?
Over the past 100 years, the number of tigers in the wild has fallen by 95 per cent to about 7000.

9

Mountain Gorillas

Mountain gorillas live in family units in the rainforests of Central Africa. They are highly endangered because of logging, poaching and war.

Threats

Logging of the rainforests opens up the land for human settlement. People move in to farm, and poachers can travel into the forest more easily.

Civil wars in Rwanda and the Democratic Republic of Congo caused people to move closer to the forests. This damaged the gorillas' habitat as people cut down trees for firewood and to build homes.

Poachers kill adult gorillas for body parts and **bushmeat**. Body parts are sold to traditional healers for medicines and to tourists as souvenirs. Captured baby gorillas have been sold as pets.

Saving the gorillas

Mountain gorillas live in national parks, so park rangers try to prevent poachers from killing the gorillas. International guidelines make it illegal to trade in live gorillas or their body parts.

The International Gorilla Conservation Programme helps to protect the gorillas by controlling the number of tourists who see them. Money from tourism helps to preserve the gorillas' habitat and, importantly is shared with the local people.

These steps seem to be working. The number of mountain gorillas in Rwanda and the Democratic Republic of Congo has increased from 324 to 380 in the past 15 years. There are only about 700 mountain gorillas in the world.

There are no mountain gorillas in zoos, only lowland gorillas like this male.

Gorilla hands have been sold as ashtrays.

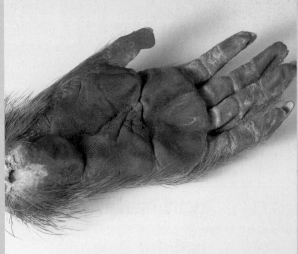

GO FACT!

DID YOU KNOW?

Mothers carry their babies in their arms until the babies are strong enough to cling to their backs.

Giant Pandas

About 1600 giant pandas live in the wild in China, and about 150 live in zoos around the world. They are endangered because their natural habitat is shrinking.

Habitat damage

In the wild, giant pandas live in **temperate** mountain forests where they have lots of bamboo to eat and trees in which to build their dens. Giant pandas spend at least 12 hours each day eating. Each giant panda needs about five square kilometres to **forage** for bamboo.

As bamboo in an area is eaten, giant pandas **migrate** to other areas. When people began settling in the giant pandas' habitat, they cut off their access to areas of bamboo. This is called **habitat fragmentation**.

Zoos and reserves

Although some giant pandas live in zoos, this is not considered good for the survival of the species because pandas do not breed well in **captivity**. As a result, the Chinese government has created nature reserves to protect the pandas and their habitats. There are habitat corridors between the nature reserves so the giant pandas can travel between them in search of bamboo.

The giant panda does not hibernate like some bears because it cannot store enough fat on a diet of only bamboo.

Giant pandas make a bleating sound similar to the sound of a lamb.

DID YOU KNOW?

The giant panda is closely related to the bear family, but scientists used to think it was a raccoon.

Endangered Sea Animals

Some sea animal species become endangered slowly, through hunting, fishing and **climate change**. Sudden threats, such as oil spills, can also kill whole communities of sea animals.

Fishing and hunting

People have always hunted sea animals for **subsistence**. When people began commercial fishing and hunting, however, animal numbers declined – some fish could not breed quickly enough to replace the fish that had been caught.

Fish endangered due to overfishing include Atlantic salmon and the Patagonian toothfish.

This has also happened to many species of sea animals, including polar bears, seals, dolphins, whales, penguins and turtles.

Warmer oceans

Climate change affects the habitats of sea animals. Global warming is melting the Arctic ice, leaving less ice for polar bears to live on. Warmer ocean temperatures also affect fish populations. If the water becomes warmer, fish do not grow as fast and are sick more often.

Pollution

Pollution affects the habitats of all species, and oil pollution at sea has an immediate and devastating effect. Oil tankers can spill their cargo because of collisions with other ships or grounding on rocks. Oil is highly toxic to fish, birds and other animals.

Rising sea temperatures, due to global warming, have increased incidents of coral bleaching, in which coral turns pale or white and may die.

Many animals, such as dolphins, die accidentally in fishing nets.

GO FACT!

DID YOU KNOW?

The oil tanker *Amoco Cadiz* ran aground off the coast of France on 16 March 1978. Its entire cargo of 227 000 tonnes of oil spilled into heavy seas. The oil contaminated 320 kilometres of coastline, and killed 20 000 sea birds and millions of **molluscs** and sea urchins. At the time, this was the largest loss of marine life ever recorded from an oil spill.

15

Penguins

Penguins are flightless sea birds that live in colonies on land and swim out to sea for food. They are severely affected by oil pollution.

Oil at sea

On 23 June 2000, a ship called *Treasure* sank near South Africa and leaked 1 300 tonnes of oil into the sea between Robben Island and Dassen Island. These islands are the homes of two of the three most important breeding colonies of the **threatened** African penguin.

About 40 000 penguins – about 40 per cent of the world's African penguin population – were in danger from this oil spill. Oil coats the penguins' feathers. This affects their ability to swim and their protection from the cold. Also, as the penguins clean their feathers they swallow oil, which is poisonous.

Cleaned and fed

To save the penguins, rescuers went to Robben Island and collected the oiled birds. They moved them to the city of Cape Town in boats and helicopters. Each bird was fed and then washed in dishwashing liquid. The clean penguins were placed in plastic pools to recover and waterproof their feathers again. When they were healthy they were released into the sea.

The oil took a few days longer to reach Dassen Island. Rescuers realised that there was no space to clean more penguins in Cape Town, so they built fences on the island to stop the penguins getting into the sea. The rescuers collected and transported all the penguins to the city of Port Elisabeth. The penguins were then released to swim 800 kilometres back home. When they got back, about three weeks later, the oil had been cleaned up.

Some penguins had to be washed more than ten times.

GO FACT!

DID YOU KNOW?

The African penguin rescue operation took three months and 90 per cent of the birds survived.

17

Polar Bears

Polar bears live mainly on ice floes in the Arctic They are not endangered now, but they are considered at risk and in need of **conservation**.

Laws of protection

Polar bears have been hunted for thousands of years by the native **Inuit** people who share their habitat. Inuit people use polar bear fur for clothing, and the meat and fat for food. They kill only what they need to survive.

Sport hunters began using aircraft and motor boats to hunt polar bears. As a result bear numbers have declined.

Governments created laws to protect the bears, and an international agreement was made to limit hunting. Now, or Inuit people are permitted to k limited number of polar bears, traditional methods, for food a clothing.

Danger in climate change

Global warming could also endanger polar bears. As the climate gets warmer, ice is melting earlier in the summer c freezing later in the winter. Pol bears spend less time on the s ice, which means they have les time to hunt seals and build ur fat reserves. This can mean female polar bears have troubl providing milk for their young. female bears don't reach a minimum weight, they won't g birth at all.

Polar bears are the largest carnivorous animals with four legs.

DID YOU KNOW?
Polar bears have black skin to retain heat. Their thick undercoat means they can overheat at temperatures above 10° Celsius.

DID YOU KNOW?
Polar bears are fantastic swimmers. They have been spotted at sea more than a kilometre from the nearest land or ice.

Sea Turtles

Sea turtles are air-breathing reptiles that live in the sea but lay their eggs on beaches. The main danger to adult turtles is drowning due to fishing practices.

Escaping predators

A female turtle always lays her eggs on the beach where she was born. The Kemp's Ridley turtle crawls onto the Rancho Nuevo Beach in Mexico, digs a hole and lays about 100 eggs. She covers the eggs with sand and returns to the sea.

There are many dangers for turtle eggs and **hatchlings**. Animal predators dig up the eggs, and people collect them.

After 45 to 60 days, the hatchlings dig their way out of the nest and crawl swiftly to the sea. Some are eaten by waiting predators, such as gulls, and some follow bright lights away from the water. If they reach the sea, the hatchlings swim very quickly until they are safe from predators.

Caught in nets

Fishing is another danger to turtles. Adult turtles travel long distances across open seas. Fishing boats often catch turtles accidentally. Turtles drown in the fishing nets because they cannot come to the surface to breathe.

To prevent this, fishing boats in the United States must use turtle excluder devices. These special trapdoors in the narrowest part of the net allow turtles to escape.

Turtle Nesting Beach

No
Horses, Fires Dogs, or Vehicles

Power Boats Are Prohibited From Landing on Beach

The turtle's strong back flippers are used for digging nests.

GO FACT!

DID YOU KNOW?

In the 1940s, 40 000 female Kemp's Ridley turtles nested in one day on a single beach in Mexico. This decreased to about 1000 in the 1980s.

Fishing nets accidentally kill many sea turtles.

There are seven species of sea turtle, such as this Hawksbill turtle. They are all endangered.

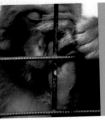

Saving Endangered Animals

Zoos and wildlife sanctuaries are working to save endangered animals from extinction. Some people think animals shouldn't be kept in zoos and that sanctuaries take up valuable land.

Saved in zoos

Zoos are places where people can see wild animals in captivity. Modern zoos educate people about animals, conduct research and encourage the conservation of endangered animals. Some animals, such as the California condor, have been saved from extinction by breeding programmes in zoos.

California condor

Trapped in zoos

Some species don't breed in captivity. Some people object to zoos because they believe it is wrong to hold animals captive. They say that zoos keep animals in poor, cramped conditions. Zoo supporters say that animals are now kept in habitats as close as possible to their natural habitat.

In the wild

You can see animals in their natural habitats in wildlife sanctuaries and national parks. Sanctuaries keep animals safe from poachers. African wildlife sanctuaries have increased the population of African elephants.

Local people sometimes object to sanctuaries being established because it can mean that they are removed from their land, or that they can no longer use the land for traditional farming or hunting.

The clouded leopard is one of the most difficult big cats to breed in captivity.

Farming has taken over more than half of the elephants' habitat in Kenya's Transmara district.

GO FACT!

ID YOU KNOW?

ellowstone National Park in the nited States was the first national ark in the world, established in 1872. he Royal National Park near Sydney, ustralia, was the second.

Tourism helps to pay for animal conservation.

Zoos are great places to learn about endangered animals and how to protect them.

Saving the Bald Eagle

The bald eagle, symbol of the United States, was threatened with extinction. Seen as pests, large numbers of them were shot or poisoned.

Poisoned birds

After World War II a **pesticide** called DDT was widely used. DDT entered the **food chain** and bald eagles ate contaminated fish. The DDT affected the eagle's eggs – the shells broke or didn't hatch. Bald eagles were also at risk because of the loss of habitat and sources of food. Eagle numbers fell dramatically, and in 1940 it was made illegal to kill or harm the bald eagle. In 1967, they were declared an endangered species.

The use of DDT was banned in 1972. People worked to conserve bald eagle habitats and breed the eagles in captivity. The Patuxent Wildlife Research Centre used the following procedure to breed bald eagles and release them where numbers were low. In 1995, the bald eagle's endangered status was downgraded to threatened.

How the bald eagle was saved

1. A captive breeding colony was established as part of a wildlife research centre.

2. The first **clutch** of eggs was removed from each nest and placed in an incubator.

3. Shredded meat was fed to the first clutch of hatchlings.

4. When the eagles laid a second clutch of eggs, they were left in the nest.

5. If more than two chicks hatched in that clutch, the extra eaglets were removed.

6. Each removed eaglet was placed with another adult pair. They raised the chick as their own.

7. Eight-week-old eaglets were returned to the wild. Enclosure were made on towers and food was provided for them.

DID YOU KNOW?

Bald eagles mate for life. In the early 1960s, there were fewer than 450 nesting pairs in the United States. In 1999, there were approximately 5800 nesting pairs.

Bald eagles often reuse their nests. Nests can be more than three metres wide and weigh around 1800 kilograms.

Bald eagles are not bald at all — they have white feathers on their heads. The name comes from the old English word 'balde', which means white.

Rhinoceroses

The rhinoceros – commonly called 'rhino' – is the second largest land mammal. There are five rhino species, all endangered by poaching. They are killed for their horns.

White rhinos

Rhino horn is made of thickly matted hair and is used in traditional medicines in Asia.

In 1885, there were only about 20 white rhinos left in southern Africa. Hunting was made illegal, and sanctuaries established to protect the rhinos. From the 1960s, white rhinos were caught and moved to wildlife sanctuaries, and some were sold to zoos around the world. There are now more than 11 000 white rhinos. As a result of careful conservation, the white rhino has been saved.

Black rhinos

Black rhino numbers declined from 1970, so that by the mid 1990s there were only 2500 left. A ban on trade in rhino horn had little effect – poachers continued to kill rhinos in national parks in Africa. They were able to do this because of civil wars in some African countries. Governments did not have control, and weapons were readily available. Today, nearly all black rhinos are guarded in small areas.

Asian rhinos

Asian rhinos remain endangered but conservation organisations are working with governments to save them. Rhino numbers in Nepal have been increasing, but poaching continues. There are fewer than 70 surviving Javan rhinos, which are in Indonesia and Vietnam.

Indian rhinos usually live alone, except for females with young.

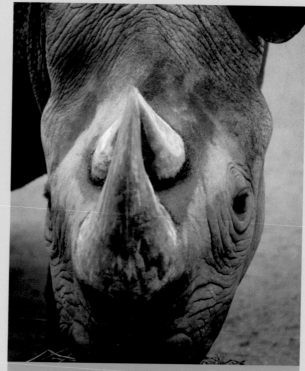

A black rhino can charge at 65 kilometres per hour

GO FACT!

DID YOU KNOW?

All rhinos are grey. The name 'white rhino' comes from an old Afrikaans word for wide (wijt) – but people thought they heard 'white'!

In the 1800s, rhino horns were crafted into ornaments, doorhandles, riding crops and walking sticks.

27

Not Saved... Yet

In the last 500 years, humans have forced 844 species to extinction. Will we ever stop?

Chimps in danger

Chimpanzees are one of the species in danger. They are our closest relative in the animal world, sharing an estimated 98 per cent of our **genes**. Chimpanzees are highly intelligent and show emotions like happiness and sadness, fear and love, yet humans threaten their future.

One hundred years ago there were almost two million chimpanzees; today, only 150 000 remain. Once found in 25 African countries, now chimpanzees are extinct in four and endangered in others because of hunting and logging.

Commitment required

Urgent action is necessary to protect the remaining chimpanzee populations. An important step is the world's first declaration on great apes, known as the Kinshasa Declaration. It was signed in 2005 by governments, scientists, environmental organisations and business groups from 27 nations. Its aim is to protect chimpanzees and other great ape species.

The Kinshasa Declaration promotes education about the great apes and greater efforts to prevent poaching. Very importantly, the declaration recognises the needs of local people — apes can help reduce poverty by increasing income from tourism.

The Kinshasa Declaration requires cooperation and commitment from many people if it is to prevent the extinction of the chimpanzee.

GO FACT!

DID YOU KNOW?

Researchers have taught chimpanzees sign language to use in conversations with each other and with humans.

Facing Extinction

Endangered species		Number	
		2000	**2004**
Frogs and toads		146	1856
Birds		1183	1213
Mammals		1130	1101
Fish		752	800
Insects		555	559
Reptiles		296	304

Glossary

bushmeat wild animals killed by hunters

captivity when an animal is kept somewhere and not allowed to leave

caviar the unfertilised eggs of various large fish, especially the sturgeon

civil war a war between groups who live in the same country

climate change the change in weather conditions due to global warming

clutch a group of eggs or hatchlings produced by the same bird

conservation managing the natural environment to make sure it is not damaged or destroyed

domestic an animal that is not wild and is kept as a pet or to produce food

endangered animals or plants which may soon not exist because there are now very few alive

extinct no longer in existence; died out

forage look for and collect food

food chain a community of species where each member is eaten in turn by another member

genes the specific chemical patterns in a cell that are received from the parents and control the development of particular characteristics in an animal or plant

global warming an increase in temperature of the Earth's atmosphere and oceans

habitat the environment in which a species naturally lives; an animal's preferred environment

habitat fragmentation when habitats that were once continuous are divided into separate fragments. It is frequently caused by humans when native vegetation is cleared for agriculture or development.

hatchling a recently hatched animal

Inuit a member of a Native American tribe who lives in the northern areas of North America and Greenland

migrate move from one habitat to another

mollusc any animal which has a soft body, no spine and is often covered with a shell, e.g. oysters, snails, clams and cuttlefish

pesticide a chemical used to kill pests, such as insects and rodents

poaching to catch and, usually, kill animals illegally

predator an animal that hunts, kills and eats other animals

species a basic classification of biology that contains organisms that look like each other and can breed with each other

subsistence managing to stay alive

temperate describes plants that grow where the weather is neither very hot nor very cold

threatened likely to become endangered in the near future

traditional medicine medical practices based on cultural beliefs, handed down from generation to generation. It may include magical rituals and herbal medicines.

Index